REMEMBERING SEVEN PROPHETS

Howard W. Hunter

REMEMBERING SEVEN PROPHETS

Howard W. Hunter

MEMORIES OF FRANCIS M. GIBBONS
AS TOLD TO DANIEL BAY GIBBONS

Sixteen Stones Press

HOLLADAY, UTAH

Copyright © 2015 by Daniel Bay Gibbons

All rights reserved. No part of this publication may be reproduced, distributed or transmitted in any form or by any means, including photocopying, recording, or other electronic or mechanical methods, without the prior written permission of the publisher, except in the case of brief quotations embodied in critical reviews and certain other noncommercial uses permitted by copyright law.

Book layout, typography, and cover design ©2015 by Julie G. Gibbons. Photo credits: all cover photographs from the private collection of Francis M. Gibbons, used by permission. Sixteen Stones Press logo design by Marina Telezar.

Sixteen Stones Press
Publisher website: www.sixteenstonespress.com

Howard W. Hunter
(Remembering Seven Prophets, Book 5)
by Daniel Bay Gibbons

Paperback ISBN 978-1-942640-14-1
eBook ISBN 978-1-942640-15-8

TABLE OF CONTENTS

Remembering Seven Prophets 1

Chronology of the Life of President Howard
W. Hunter... 5

"A home of books with a piano in the
center"... 15

"We don't appreciate your playing ragtime
music" 17

"Church leaders who were lawyers"..................... 19

"The circumstances of his call to the
Apostleship" 21

"Think" 25

"A sweet, hopeful, and ncomplaining
attitude" 27

"A loving husband" 29

"President Hunters wisdom and vision were
vindicated".. 31

"He was uniformly kind to everyone" 33

"The fourth junior member of the Twelve" 34

"How Prophets are raised up"............................. 37

"The first time I have seen three stake
presidents in agreement" 40

"A sweet and kind a spirit about him" 42

"Very cordial and quite passive" 44

"He took great delight in children" 46

"The unity that exists among the highest leaders" 48

"A man wholly without guile" 49

"The Church is a friend to Islam" 51

"Absolute faith in the blessings of the Priesthood" 53

"The timetable of the Lord" 55

"LeGrand will yet return and sit in this chair!" 57

About the Author 59

Index 60

REMEMBERING SEVEN PROPHETS

This collection of reminiscences about the life of President Howard W. Hunter, the fourteenth President of The Church of Jesus Christ of Latter-day Saints is part of a larger work entitled *Remembering Seven Prophets*. This work is the fruit of more than eighty hours of interviews I conducted with my father, Francis M. Gibbons, between the years 2001 to 2011, and then another dozen hours of interviews conducted between July and December of 2014 following my return from presiding over the Russia Novosibirsk Mission of the Church.

"A Plutarch to the Presidents of the Church"

Now in his ninety-fourth year, Francis M. Gibbons is perhaps the greatest student on the lives of the Presidents of the Church in this dispensation. He has two unique qualifications to speak and write about the Prophets.

First, over the past forty-five years, my father has become "a Plutarch to the Presidents of the Church." This unusual phrase has reference to Plutarch, the ancient Greek writer, who became the most famous biographer in history, the "Father of Biography." Many years ago my father shared with my mother his special aspiration to become "a Plutarch to the Presidents of the Church, and through their lives to write the history of the Church." If any man or woman deserves the title "Plutarch to the Presidents of the Church," it is my father, Francis M. Gibbons. Over the past four decades he has become by far the most prolific writer of biographies of the Presidents of the Church, writing a full-length biography of every Prophet from Joseph Smith to Gordon B. Hinckley. Dad's biographies of the Prophets have been very popular, selling many hundreds of thousands of copies. Thirteen of his presidential biographies have been included in Brigham Young University's list of "Sixty Significant Mormon Biographies." He has truly become "a Plutarch to the Presidents of the Church."

"A Scribe to the Prophets"

Second, my father has been a personal witness and observer of the character of the last seven Presidents of the Church:

Presidents Joseph Fielding Smith, Harold B. Lee, Spencer W. Kimball, Ezra Taft Benson, Howard W. Hunter, Gordon B. Hinckley, and Thomas S. Monson. He knew these men personally. He worked with them. While serving from 1970 to 1986 as the secretary to the First Presidency and later as a member of the Seventy, Dad associated with them on a daily basis. He was a "Scribe to the Prophets," as were William Clayton, Wilford Woodruff, Joseph F. Smith, William F. Gibbons, Joseph Anderson, and others before him.

"I am their witness"

When Dad was sustained as a General Authority in April of 1986, after many years serving as the faithful scribe for the Presidents of the Church, he said:

> The Church is led by prophets, seers and revelators. I am their witness. I testify that they are honorable, upright, dedicated men of integrity, committed to teaching the principles of the gospel, who strive with all of their might to prepare a people ready for the return of the head of the Church, Jesus Christ, at His second coming.

REMEMBERING SEVEN PROPHETS

This work, *Remembering Seven Prophets*, shares many unique stories, anecdotes, insights, and testimonies about the last seven Presidents of the Church, which are nowhere else available.

I offer this work for the enlightenment and inspiration of the reader and as a tribute to the memory of the seven Presidents of the Church featured in these pages. I love and honor these great men, and add my witness to that of my father that they were and are Prophets of God!

Daniel Bay Gibbons
August 3, 2015
Holladay, Utah

CHRONOLOGY OF THE LIFE OF PRESIDENT HOWARD W. HUNTER

November 14, 1907
Howard W. Hunter is born in Salt Lake City, Utah, to John William Hunter and Nellie Rasmussen Hunter.

April 4, 1920
President Howard W. Hunter is baptized in Boise, Idaho at age twelve.

June 1926
President Howard W. Hunter graduates from high school in Boise, Idaho, and begins a career as a professional pianist and bandleader. He puts together a five-man combo called "Hunter's Croonaders."

January 5, 1927
President Howard W. Hunter and "Hunters Croonaders" embark from Seattle, Washington, on the *SS President Jackson*, a cruise ship, for an extended tour of the Far East, with the band providing evening music for the entertainment of the passengers.

March 1928
President Howard W. Hunter decides to move to Los Angeles, California, and begins taking night classes at the American Institute of Banking while continuing his musical career. He also meets his future wife, Clara May Jeffs, in his LDS ward in Los Angeles.

June 6, 1931
President Howard W. Hunter plays his last engagement as a professional musician. That night he packs up his professional band instruments and never uses them again. Four days later, on **June 10, 1931**, he is married and sealed to Clara Jeffs in the Salt Lake Temple.

October 1934
President Howard W. Hunter's first son, Howard William Hunter, Jr., dies when he is seven months old.

September 1935
President Howard W. Hunter is admitted as a law student at Southwestern University.

June 1939
President Howard W. Hunter graduates *cum laude* from Southwestern University College of Law. Soon thereafter he sits for and passes the California bar exam.

1940
President Howard W. Hunter rents an office and opens a solo law practice.

August 1940
President Howard W. Hunter is surprised to be called as bishop of the El Sereno Ward. He serves for six years.

November 1946
President Howard W. Hunter is called as the president of the stake high priests quorum.

1948
President Howard W. Hunter buys a new home in Arcadia, California.

February 1950
President Howard W. Hunter is called as president of the Pasadena Stake. He serves for nine and a half years.

REMEMBERING SEVEN PROPHETS

October 9, 1959
President Howard W. Hunter is surprised to be called as a member of the Quorum of the Twelve by President David O. McKay. He is sustained **October 10, 1959** and ordained and set apart the following Thursday, **October 15, 1959**.

October 1959 to April 1961
President Howard W. Hunter winds down his law practice in California, traveling by train or plane each week to Salt Lake City to attend the Thursday council meetings of the First Presidency and Quorum of the Twelve.

April 1961
President Howard W. Hunter and his family move into an apartment in Salt Lake City.

Late 1961
President and Sister Hunter travel to the Middle East with President and Sister Spencer W. Kimball. They visit Iraq, Egypt, the Holy Land, Europe, and Great Britain.

July 22, 1963
President Howard W. Hunter and his family move into a newly constructed home in the Oak Hills subdivision of Salt Lake City.

January 1964
President Howard W. Hunter becomes president of the Genealogical Society.

January 1965
President Howard W. Hunter is appointed president and chairman of the board of the Church's Polynesian Cultural Center in Hawaii.

June 22, 1966
President Howard W. Hunter dedicates the newly constructed Granite Mountain Record Vaults of the Church in Little Cottonwood Canyon near Salt Lake City.

August 1969
President Howard W. Hunter directs the World Conference on Records held in Salt Lake City.

REMEMBERING SEVEN PROPHETS

January 1970
President Howard W. Hunter is appointed Church Historian and Recorder following the death of President David O. McKay.

November 1975
President Howard W. Hunter creates fifteen stakes out of five in a single weekend in Mexico City, Mexico.

1981 to 1982
President Howard W. Hunter's wife, Clara May Jeffs Hunter, suffers several cerebral hemorrhages and is moved to a nursing care facility where she spends the remainder of her life.

October 1983
President Howard W. Hunter's first wife, Clara May Jeffs Hunter, passes away after a long illness.

November 1985
President Howard W. Hunter becomes Acting President of the Quorum of the Twelve upon the death of President Spencer W. Kimball. A few years later, after the death of President

Marion G. Romney, President Hunter is set apart as President of the Quorum.

October 1986
President Howard W. Hunter undergoes quadruple-bypass surgery.

October 1987
President Howard W. Hunter delivers his first sermon in General Conference while seated in a wheelchair.

May 20, 1988
President Howard W. Hunter becomes President of the Quorum of the Twelve Apostles following the death of President Marion G. Romney.

May 1989
President Howard W. Hunter travels to the Holy Land to attend the dedication of the Jerusalem Center.

April 10, 1990
President Howard W. Hunter is married and sealed to his second wife, Inis Stanton, in the Salt Lake Temple.

REMEMBERING SEVEN PROPHETS

September 12, 1992
President Howard W. Hunter dedicates Austria for the preaching of the Gospel.

February 1993
President Howard W. Hunter is threatened by an assailant in the BYU Marriott Center in Provo, Utah.

May 30, 1994
President Howard W. Hunter becomes the senior Apostle upon the death of President Ezra Taft Benson.

June 5, 1994
President Howard W. Hunter is ordained and set apart as the fourteenth President of the Church.

1994 to 1995
Shortly after succeeding to the Prophetic office, President Howard W. Hunter presides over ceremonies in Nauvoo, Illinois, commemorating the 150th anniversary of the martyrdom of Joseph and Hyrum Smith. President Hunter creates the two thousandth stake of the Church in Mexico City, and he

dedicates temples in Orlando, Florida, and Bountiful, Utah.

January 1995
President Howard W. Hunter is hospitalized with bone cancer.

March 3, 1995
President Howard W. Hunter passes away at his home in Salt Lake City, with his wife, Inis, by his side.

"A HOME OF BOOKS WITH A PIANO IN THE CENTER"

President Howard W. Hunter grew up in Boise, Idaho, in a loving home environment. His father was not a member of the Church, while his mother was a believing Latter-day Saint. My impression is that President Hunter learned qualities of faith from his mother and independent thinking from his father. As a boy, President Hunter was disposed to go his own way and keep his own counsel. President Hunter's father would not allow his son to be baptized at age eight, but insisted he wait longer to make sure the boy was certain about the course of action he wanted to take. The father finally relented when he saw young Howard's disappointment in not being advanced to the Aaronic Priesthood with his friends at age twelve.

President Hunter grew up in a home of books with a piano in the center. He once told me that his father loved books, and their home in Boise was filled with good literature. There was also a piano in the home, which President Hunter was encouraged to play. Both of these resources—a home library and the family piano—became crucial tools for the growth and development of young Howard W. Hunter. He became a reading man very early in his life, and this inclination stayed with him throughout his youth, his legal and business career, and his life as an Apostle and ultimately President of the Church. The piano also was a crucial tool—in fact, President Hunter's first dream was to pursue a career in music. He learned to play several other instruments besides the piano, and as a teenager embarked on the life of a professional performing musician. Though he later abandoned this path, he was a lifelong lover of music, and even into his high old age he could play the piano with great skill and feeling.

"WE DON'T APPRECIATE YOUR PLAYING RAGTIME MUSIC"

Sister Gibbons and I once had dinner with President Howard W. Hunter and his wife, during which he shared these revealing anecdotes related to his youth:

President Hunter told us about the band he formed after finishing high school and his efforts to make his way as a professional musician for several years. This was in the late 1920's and early 1930's, and he was very skilled on the piano and also very much into the popular music of the day. He told us that one evening he was at a gathering of young Latter-day Saints in the home of a Brother Ursenbach, who lived in his home ward in Boise, Idaho. President Hunter was the life of the party, as he sat at the Ursenbach's piano and played popular songs while the youth and young singles gathered around, singing along with him and applauding him. Apparently this rankled the very staid and conservative Brother Ursenbach, who, at the end of the evening, said to President Hunter: "We enjoy having you in our home, but we don't appreciate your playing ragtime music on our piano!"

During this period the young President Hunter traveled throughout the Pacific and Far East with his band called "Hunter's Croonaders." Later, he returned home to pursue his education and find his niche in the world. But President Hunter told us that he continued to play with his band at professional gigs for several years to help fund his education. He would play dance music in clubs until late at night, then study during the day. This was during the period when he was courting and ultimately preparing to marry his first wife, Clara May Jeffs. He told us that after the wedding had been set and all the preparations made to travel to the Salt Lake Temple to be sealed, President Hunter played one final gig with his band. The group played at a dance until about 2:00 in the morning. Afterward, he went home, carefully cleaned and stored his band instruments, and then never used them again, except on rare special family occasions.

"Church leaders who were lawyers"

Of all the Prophets I have known personally and worked with, President Howard W. Hunter had the most unique personality. Perhaps part of this difference arises from the fact that he is the only lawyer among all of the Presidents of the Church. I have often thought that some of the early brethren, Brigham Young in particular, might have expressed dismay that a lawyer had risen to the Prophetic office. As a lawyer, President Hunter had a unique training, not shared by any other President of the Church. To be sure, there have been other prominent Church leaders who were lawyers, including First Presidency counselors Presidents J. Reuben Clark, Hugh B. Brown, Henry D. Moyle, Stephen L. Richards, and James E. Faust. Other lawyers in the highest echelons of Church leadership have included Elders Bruce R. McConkie, Dallin H. Oaks, D. Todd Christopherson, and others. But up until now, we have had only a single lawyer serve as the

REMEMBERING SEVEN PROPHETS

President of the Church—President Howard W. Hunter.

"THE CIRCUMSTANCES OF HIS CALL TO THE APOSTLESHIP"

Over a period of sixteen years I had the almost daily privilege of observing President Hunter in his work at Church headquarters. However, I gained additional insight into his character and personality when he was assigned in the early 1970's as a conference visitor in the Bonneville Stake, over which I presided. It was most interesting to spend time with him away from headquarters.

After he received the conference assignment, he visited with me about the preparations for the conference. During that discussion I told him that it was conceivable that both President Spencer W. Kimball and President Marion G. Romney might be in attendance, as they both lived within the boundaries of the stake. Hearing this, President Hunter joked, "I hope they don't come!" He then told me that it must be tough presiding over a stake where the Prophet and so many other General Authorities resided. "You must have the feeling that they are constantly looking over your shoulder," he said.

During the weekend of stake conference, I had a long and relaxed visit with President Hunter. He related to me the circumstances of his call to the Apostleship.

Before his call as a General Authority, President Hunter had been a stake president in Pasadena, California, where was a prominent practicing attorney and businessman. He thus came from a background far removed from Church headquarters, but traveled each General Conference to attend the sessions as a stake president. He told me that he flew to Salt Lake City in the morning with one of his counselors, Daken K. Broadhead. They checked into the Hotel Utah and were able to attend the last part of the morning session. After the morning session, President Hunter lingered in the Tabernacle to visit with some acquaintances and then returned to the hotel to freshen up before the afternoon session.

When President Hunter arrived at his hotel room and began to unlock the door, his counselor, Daken Broadhead, who occupied an adjoining room, came out into the hallway and said, "Claire Middlemiss, President David O. McKay's secretary called. She is looking for you!"

"All right," said President Hunter, not feeling any particular excitement about the phone call. "I'll call her."

Daken said, "Aren't you at all excited or curious about this?"

"Why should I be," asked President Hunter.

Daken answered, "There's a vacancy in the Quorum of the Twelve, you know."

"Oh come on, Daken!" said President Hunter.

A short while later President Hunter presented himself at 47 East South Temple and was immediately ushered into President David O. McKay's office. He said that the Prophet took President Hunter into his arms and said, in substance, "Brother Hunter, the Lord has spoken. You have been called as a member of the Quorum of the Twelve. Your ministry will now extend to the entire world!"

President Hunter told me that he couldn't remember anything the Prophet said after those initial shocking words. In fact, he said, he remembers very little of anything that transpired between receiving his calling and being sustained in General Conference the following day. He did remember attending a basketball game with his son that evening and then wandering in a daze on a long walk through the streets of downtown Salt Lake City and up Capitol Hill, where he sat and meditated for hours on the grounds of the State Capitol.

President Hunter told me that he had no premonition of any kind of his call to the Twelve.

"Think"

President Howard W. Hunter was a reading man. I understand that his boyhood home was filled with books, as were his homes in California and Salt Lake City. His office at 47 East South Temple was also filled with books of Church history and biography, as well as the classics of world literature. The scriptures were invariably open upon the desk in his office.

I remember being with President Hunter in his office one day when I remarked upon something I had often noticed on his credenza—a little plaque that had the word, "Think" engraved upon it. I asked him about the significance of this. He told me that as a young man and a practicing lawyer he had always been greatly impressed by the writings of James Allen, the popular author of *As a Man Thinketh*, and Napoleon Hill, the author of *Think and Grow Rich*. This accounted for this visual reminder, which he always had on his desk. More than any of the Brethren I was blessed to know, President Howard W. Hunter knew how to "think."

REMEMBERING SEVEN PROPHETS

It is interesting to contrast this little office motto with that of President Hunter's predecessor, President Spencer W. Kimball. President Kimball had a similar plaque on his office desk with the motto, "Do it." I think that these mottos say something about the personal style and focus of these two great Prophets of God! Both careful thought as well as concrete action are important.

"A SWEET, HOPEFUL, AND UNCOMPLAINING ATTITUDE"

In the late 1970's President Howard W. Hunter began to suffer from various physical problems. I remember that the first indication of his coming physical ordeals appeared when he contracted the mumps. President Hunter was on the receiving end of a great deal of good-natured kidding and banter among the leading Brethren of the Church when this happened—after all, mumps is an illness we typically associate with children, not men in their seventies! However, it soon became apparent that the mumps were no laughing matter for President Hunter, and he developed serious complications. President Hunter received several administrations from the First Presidency during this time and became the subject of daily, fervent prayers spoken in his behalf.

After several months, President Hunter underwent abdominal surgery to remove a benign tumor. Then, while he was recovering from the surgery, he suffered a heart attack. Over the next several years President Hunter endured a litany of physical ailments:

continued heart problems, the deterioration of his spinal discs, bleeding ulcers, and the loss of much of the use of his legs. All of this he endured with a sweet, hopeful, and uncomplaining attitude.

"A LOVING HUSBAND"

President Howard W. Hunter's first wife, Clara May Jeffs Hunter began to suffer severe headaches and memory loss in the early 1970's, when she was still a relatively young woman. She was the subject of many blessings during that time, and her name was a near-constant fixture on the special prayer roll of the First Presidency and Quorum of the Twelve for their regular Thursday meetings for the last decade of her life. Sister Hunter's condition worsened over the years, and ultimately she became virtually incapacitated. In the early 1980's she suffered several cerebral hemorrhages, and it was necessary for her to have twenty-four hour care in a nursing facility from that time forward. She ultimately passed away in October of 1983.

It was inspiring to observe President Hunter during these years. He visited Claire faithfully each day while she was in the nursing home, and sometimes twice a day. When he was with her, he would sit and talk quietly with her. Even though she could not speak, she could express herself through facial expressions or the squeeze of a hand. I understand that she was generally unresponsive to her nurses or other family members or friends who visited her, and that she only responded to President Hunter.

"PRESIDENT HUNTERS WISDOM AND VISION WERE VINDICATED"

President Howard W. Hunter was a true visionary and also a bold administrator, even in the face of doubters. In November of 1975, during the administration of President Kimball, President Hunter, then in the Twelve, was assigned to travel to Mexico City to divide the five fast-growing stakes located there. He was given broad discretion by the First Presidency to divide the stakes as he saw fit, but it was envisioned that this might result in an increase of three, four, or perhaps five new stakes. However, once he was on the ground, President Hunter made the decision to create fifteen stakes out of five! This he accomplished with the help of Elder J. Thomas Fyans, an Assistant to the Quorum of the Twelve, and several Regional Representatives.

When word came back to Church headquarters that President Hunter had created fifteen stakes, there were mixed feelings on the part of some of the Brethren. A few felt that he had overstepped his bounds and spread the organization too thinly. However, President Hunter's wisdom and vision were vindicated, as all fifteen of the new stakes thrived, and in fact had to be divided again in less than two years.

"He was uniformly kind to everyone"

When I first met President Hunter I was immediately impressed by his warmth and friendliness. He was very open and approachable. He did not seem to have an inflated sense of his own importance. Though I was in a subservient position, he always treated me with the utmost respect and dignity. He was uniformly kind to everyone—to both those above him and those below him. He was highly intelligent, but not necessarily an intellectual. He was positive and quick in his actions and very pleasant and open-faced in his dealings. It was evident to me from the outset that here was a man of deep faith who could be trusted.

"THE FOURTH JUNIOR MEMBER OF THE TWELVE"

I first met Howard W. Hunter in the Upper Room of the temple on April 9, 1970. That was the first day I attended a meeting of the Council of the First Presidency and the Twelve in the Upper Room of the Salt Lake Temple. Earlier that day I had attended my first meeting of the First Presidency in the Council Room on the main floor of the Church Administration Building. At the time I was a practicing attorney in Salt Lake City and had the surprising experience of being invited that Thursday morning to meet with the Prophet and his counselors. During that meeting, it was decided by the First Presidency that I was to replace Elder Joseph Anderson as the Secretary to the First Presidency.

The First Presidency, consisting of Presidents Joseph Fielding Smith, Harold B. Lee, and N. Eldon Tanner, left the Administration Building just before 10:00 that morning. Joseph Anderson and I accompanied them, and we walked to the temple through the tunnel beneath Main Street.

When we got to the temple, we took the elevator up to the fourth floor and had entered what is called the "Upper Room," or the Council Room of the First Presidency and the Quorum of the Twelve. There, each Thursday for more than a century, the First Presidency and the Twelve have met to guide the Church. Prior to the construction of the Salt Lake Temple, the Brethren met in other places, dating back to the days of Joseph Smith in Nauvoo, when weekly prayer meetings were held with the Twelve and other Church leaders each Thursday.

As we entered the Upper Room, the Twelve, who had been in session there since 8:00 a.m., stood in order to shake hands with the Brethren. President Lee took me around the semi-circle and introduced me personally to each member of the Twelve. I had previously met only two of them—Elder Delbert L. Stapley, whom I had known in Phoenix, and Elder Richard L. Evans, whom I had known from my service as a guide on Temple Square and who had recently ordained me as the Bishop of the Yalecrest Ward in the Bonneville Stake. The others, of course, I knew by reputation.

REMEMBERING SEVEN PROPHETS

At the time I first shook hands with President Howard W. Hunter, he was the fourth junior member of the Twelve, being senior only to Elders Gordon B. Hinckley, Thomas S. Monson and Boyd K. Packer. Elder Packer, incidentally, was ordained and set apart as a member of the Twelve later in the meeting.

As I shook hands with President Hunter, he greeted me warmly with a genuine smile. I learned later he had questioned taking me away from the legal profession at such a relatively young age when I had reached the point of greatest influence and productivity as an attorney. Being an attorney himself, he would have appreciated my status and situation more than any of the others.

"How Prophets are raised up"

Not long after commencing my duties as the secretary to the First Presidency, I accompanied the Brethren to St. George, Utah, where a Solemn Assembly was held in the St. George Temple. We all rode down on a chartered bus. En route, we stopped in Provo, where Brother Dallin H. Oaks, the future Apostle, was installed as the new president of the Brigham Young University. By then, President Hunter had been appointed as the Church Historian and Recorder. This was a position he cherished, as he had been an avid record keeper since the days of his youth when he commenced to keep a diary in Boise, Idaho. On the way to St. George, I noticed him making careful notes, perhaps for his own diary or for the official church record.

In St. George, the night before the Solemn Assembly was to begin, the party was served dinner in one of the local ward recreation halls. Afterward the Brethren went to their own quarters, either to sleep or to prepare for the morrow. Instead of going to bed immediately, I decided to take a walk up Main Street. On the way back, I met President

Hunter, who also was out for a constitutional. We fell in together and spent about a half hour visiting as we walked. It was the first time I really had a chance to talk to him on a personal basis. I found him to be open, friendly, and devoid of any sense of self-importance or arrogance. There was no guile in him. In the years ahead I saw and heard nothing that was inconsistent with these first impressions of Howard W. Hunter.

During this same trip, I had a long private conversation with Elder Gordon B. Hinckley in Fillmore, Utah. He told me about his grandfather, Ira Hinckley who built Cove Fort and who later was the President of the Millard Stake with headquarters in Fillmore. It was a coincidence that on this the first trip I took with the Brethren I had private conversations with two members of the Twelve who would later become Presidents of the Church.

It is interesting to consider the vastly different backgrounds of these two future Presidents of the Church: President Hunter was born in Boise, Idaho, of a father who was not a member of the church and who would not allow Howard to be baptized until he was over twelve years of age. Even then he relented only because President Hunter was crushed because he could not pass the sacrament with his friends. On the other hand, Elder Hinckley's father, Bryant S. Hinckley, and grandfather, Ira Hinckley, were both stake presidents. And his father was a confidant of President Heber J. Grant, wrote his biography, handled some of his personal correspondence, and made behind-the-scene contacts for him.

Encouraged by his family, Elder Hinckley graduated from the University and filled a mission while at the same age President Hunter organized a band called "Hunter's Croonaders" and took it on an extended luxury ship cruise of the orient. He later had to complete his university legal studies by attending night school while working full time. It is a classic example of how Prophets are raised up from widely different environments but with the same dedication to the Lord and His Church.

"THE FIRST TIME I HAVE SEEN THREE STAKE PRESIDENTS IN AGREEMENT"

While I served as a stake president in Salt Lake City, I had an interesting interchange with President Hunter. Marvin Curtis, president of the Monument Park Stake; Lamonte Peterson, president of the Salt Lake Central Stake; and I as president of the Bonneville Stake had conferred about recommending boundary changes affecting the three stakes. What we had come up with was to transfer the Monument Park Second Ward and that portion of the Monument Park First Ward below the Boulevard from the Monument Park Stake to the Bonneville Stake; and to transfer the Douglas Ward, the Thirty-Third Ward and the North Thirty Third Ward from the Bonneville Stake to the Salt Lake Central Stake. Interestingly, the effect of these changes was to transfer President Kimball and President Romney from the Monument Park Stake to the Bonneville Stake and to transfer President Tanner from the Bonneville Stake to the Salt Lake Central Stake.

In any event, when these recommendations were submitted to Church headquarters, President Howard W. Hunter was assigned to study the matter and to make a report and recommendation. President Hunter conferred with the three of us, reviewed the maps and the documents, and concluded it was the thing to do. When he made his report in the temple meeting, where the changes were approved, he said in substance, "Because this is the first time I have seen three stake presidents in full agreement on a matter, I recommend the application be approved without question."

"A SWEET AND KIND A SPIRIT ABOUT HIM"

I have mentioned elsewhere that the First Presidency and the Quorum of the Twelve hold a council meeting each Thursday in the Salt Lake Temple. The Brethren sit in fifteen large chairs in a circle during these meetings, in order of seniority, with the members of the First Presidency sitting at the head of the circle, and the Twelve Apostles sitting around the circle in order of seniority. Beside the chair of the junior Apostle is a small writing desk, which I was privileged to occupy during these meetings, taking shorthand minutes of the proceedings. These meetings were usually many hours long, often lasting from early morning into the early or even late afternoon. Following each meeting the Brethren ate a meal together in a special dining room on the fourth floor of the temple. This meal was served "family style," with the food laid out in large serving dishes in the center of the table, which the Brethren helped themselves to or passed around as you might do in a simple evening meal in any Latter-day Saint home. It was another one of my great privileges to join the fifteen members of the First Presidency and the Twelve for these weekly luncheons in the temple. The members of the First Presidency and Twelve invariably took their seats around the large dining room table in order of seniority.

For many years President Howard W. Hunter sat beside Elder LeGrand Richards in meetings of the Twelve or in conference settings, and also at this dining table on the fourth floor of the Temple. Elder Richards was quite elderly during the time I knew and served with him, while President Hunter was still in his early sixties, a generation younger than the older Apostle. It was inspiring for me to observe President Hunter in his interaction with Elder Richards and the other Apostles at these dinner settings. President Hunter had as sweet and kind a spirit about him as any of the Brethren I have ever known. At the luncheons following the council meetings, President Hunter was invariably the first one in the dining room, where he began pouring ice water in the glasses of the arriving Brethren. He was also very solicitous of Elder Richards, who sat next to him at the table, to make certain that his needs were cared for.

"VERY CORDIAL AND QUITE PASSIVE"

After my call as a General Authority, I was assigned to travel to a stake conference as a junior companion to President Howard W. Hunter. The stake presidency was reorganized during the conference we attended together. During the interviews we conducted, he was very cordial and quite passive. He did not lead out aggressively in the conversations, as some are prone to do. Instead, he allowed them to develop and to proceed in a normal way. Indeed, when one left the room he probably would not have known he had been interviewed, except for the fact he had been told he was coming for an interview.

During the time we were together, I sought to draw President Hunter out to gain helpful insights into him and into other General Authorities with whom he had worked. I was especially interested in President Hunter's anecdote about the Apostle, Elder Joseph F. Merrill, who was a conference visitor to the Pasadena Stake while President Hunter was the stake president. After the conference, Howard accompanied the visitor to the depot to catch his train. When Elder Merrill started walking toward a chair car, his host tried to steer him toward the Pullman. The apostle continued toward the chair car, explaining, "I always take the chair car to Las Vegas then transfer to a Pullman. Doing this saves the church $11.50." This is typical of other stories I have heard about the frugality and honesty of Elder Merrill.

"HE TOOK GREAT DELIGHT IN CHILDREN"

President Howard W. Hunter always took great delight in children and had a special feeling for the young people of the Church. I recall while he served as a member of the Twelve he delighted in sharing stories about children in the Church, which he heard as he traveled about the world. For example, during the administration of President Harold B. Lee he took special pleasure in recounting the story of a Primary child, who told his mother that the children had been singing a special song about the Prophet at the commencement of Primary each week. When the mother asked what the song was, the child began singing, "Reverent-Lee, Quiet-Lee!"

On another occasion President Hunter shared this delightful story: An announcement was made in a stake where President Hunter was to hold a conference that "Apostle Hunter" would be attending and speaking. A little boy who heard this announcement in Primary went home and excitedly told his parents that "A Possum Hunter" would be speaking at stake conference!

On still another occasion, President Hunter told of this experience. He was greeting the saints after a particularly long meeting, when he saw a young boy lingering in the chapel waiting for his parents. President Hunter caught the eye of the boy and called to him, asking him how he enjoyed the meeting. The boy's honest answer delighted President Hunter. "Well," he said, "When I sit so long, I don't hear so good."

"THE UNITY THAT EXISTS AMONG THE HIGHEST LEADERS"

Early in my association with President Hunter, I had a long discussion with him about the extraordinary operation of the leading councils of the Church. At the time, President Hunter had been a member of the Twelve for over a decade. He confided in me that in all his time at Church headquarters he had never seen a dissenting vote on any matter that came before the First Presidency and the Twelve for decision. He went on to say that this was no indication of a lack of diversity of opinion. To the contrary. He said that the members of the Twelve and the First Presidency were all very strong men with firm opinions. But, he said, as matters were discussed and debated by the Brethren, one was able to judge how the consensus of opinion was lining up, and this was how the Brethren voted. It was, he said, a testimony to the unity that exists among the highest leaders of the Church.

"A MAN WHOLLY WITHOUT GUILE"

I was in the home of President Howard W. Hunter only once. It was in about 1980, when President Kimball was recuperating from one of his many illnesses. I had accompanied Presidents Tanner and Romney to President Kimball's home, where a First Presidency meeting was held. At the time, President Hunter also was recuperating from an illness, or perhaps it was a surgery. Since the Hunters' home was only a few blocks from the Prophet's residence, we decided to call on him before returning to the office. President Hunter's wife, Claire, was then in a full care facility, so he was home alone. We had called ahead to make sure it would not be inconvenient to visit him. We found President Hunter dressed in slacks, a shirt open at the collar, stockings and house slippers, and a handsome house robe. The house was immaculate. Nothing seemed out of place. The airy living room where we chatted was tastefully decorated in light hues. Crystal chandeliers could be seen in the adjoining dining room and a large piece of statuary occupied a prominent place in the living room.

REMEMBERING SEVEN PROPHETS

As always, President Hunter was cordial and gracious. He had a pleasant smile, and when he was amused, he had a subdued but genuine chuckle. We visited, talking shop, asking about his health, and reporting on the condition of the Prophet, then left. The visit confirmed my impression of President Hunter as a man wholly without guile, humble, and sincere, yet a man assured of his own self worth. There was a sweet spirit in his home, a spirit of peace and contentment.

In council meetings, President Hunter said little, unlike other members of the Twelve, who spoke out on almost every issue. When President Hunter did speak, however, his words had impact and were listened to. In reporting assignments, he related only positive things. Like a good lawyer, he chose his words carefully. And he used them with telling effect.

His most enduring contribution to the Mormon community was his admonition to live Christlike lives, to be loving and kind to each other, and to make the temple the earthly object of our energies and devotion.

"The Church is a Friend to Islam"

President Hunter was a very tolerant and open-minded man. An example of this occurred during the 1970's, when he befriended three young Arab students who were living in Salt Lake City and attending the University of Utah. One day President Hunter invited these three students and their advisor to 47 East South Temple and introduced them to President Spencer W. Kimball, then President of the Church. The three young men were very eloquent and well spoken and made a favorable impression with President Kimball. I was with Presidents Hunter and Kimball as they visited with these young men, who were pleading with the Prophet for a more balanced stance of the Church toward Muslims generally, and Palestinians in particular. President Kimball and President Hunter told them that the Church is a friend to Islam and its people and takes seriously their divine commission to preach the gospel to all, including Muslims.

It was inspiring to see these two servants of the Lord testify to these young men about their apostolic commissions to carry the gospel to all nations, including to the nations of Islam.

"Absolute faith in the blessings of the Priesthood"

In the mid 1970's President Hunter told me this remarkable story:

During his apostolic service, President Hunter toured the South Pacific and visited a remote island where a stalwart group of Latter-day Saints lived. He said the conditions on the island were very primitive, but the people seemed happy beyond measure and possessed with a deep spirituality and hope in the promises of the gospel. One day near the conclusion of his visit to this island, a Latter-day Saint couple approached President Hunter and asked for a special blessing. Through a translator, the wife explained to the Apostle that she had been barren for many years and unable to bear children, but that she and her husband had hopes of having a child to raise in the gospel. President Hunter complied with their request and gave the woman a blessing.

Nine months after his return to Salt Lake City, President Hunter received word through the mission president that this woman had conceived and borne a child. Four years later he received the news through another source that this woman had conceived again and bore a second child. About this time, Elder Marvin J. Ashton of the Twelve visited this same island and this same woman asked him for a blessing. He complied, and word later came to President Hunter and Elder Ashton that this believing woman had conceived a third time, and nine months later bore a set of twins.

President Hunter seemed deeply moved by this story. He said it was a powerful illustration in the principle of faith. This sister had absolute faith in the blessings of the priesthood, and she was blessed for it.

"THE TIMETABLE OF THE LORD"

In late 1983 President Hunter traveled on Church business to the Middle East in company with Elder Mark E. Peterson of the Quorum of the Twelve. During this trip, the Brethren were involved in a terrible automobile accident near Cairo, Egypt, and Elder Peterson was gravely injured. It was undoubtedly as a result of these injuries that Elder Peterson's life was shortened. He ultimately died in January of 1984.

President Hunter later shared with me these details about the accident: President Hunter and Elder Peterson were traveling together with several others in two vehicles. At the last moment before their departure, President Hunter was about to enter one vehicle with Elder Peterson, when he urged him to ride in the second vehicle. A short while later, a drunken motorist crossed over the median strip of a divided highway and crashed almost head-on into the car in which Elder Peterson was riding.

This experience is a good illustration of the truth that we never know the precise timetable of the Lord, but have faith that if we are faithful we are in His hands, both in life and in death. President Hunter did not ascribe any special Providence to this experience, but I can't help but feel that the Lord had his hand in preserving the life of this future President of the Church.

"LeGrand will yet return and sit in this chair!"

In the early 1980's, Brother William O. Nelson, who served for many years as an assistant secretary to the Quorum of the Twelve, told me this story about President Hunter:

Two or three years before he died, Elder LeGrand Richards of the Quorum of the Twelve was gravely ill and not expected to live. In fact, his doctors told Elder Richards' family that the end was very near and that they should prepare themselves. This grave diagnosis was reported to the members of the Quorum of the Twelve, and in one of their meetings the Brethren spent a significant period of time talking about Elder Richards and extolling his virtues and past contributions. President Hunter was next to Elder Richards in seniority, and so always sat next to him in council meetings. Bill said that some of the Brethren expressed regret that Elder Richards would no longer be with them.

During all this time President Hunter sat quietly by, sitting in his arm chair next to Elder Richards' empty seat, but finally spoke up and said quietly, "Brethren, LeGrand isn't dead yet." This comment was ignored, and the other Brethren continued their eulogies. Finally, President Hunter brought his hands down on the arms of his chair in an unusual show of forcefulness, and pointing to the empty chair beside him said, "Brethren! LeGrand will yet return and sit in this chair!"

Within a short time Elder Richards recovered fully and returned to very vigorous service in the Twelve and continued on for several years. In fact, it was after this experience that Elder Richards experienced the remarkable appearance of President Wilford Woodruff in the Upper Room of the Temple in connection with the 1978 revelation on Priesthood.

This experience reveals both the spirituality of President Hunter as well as his quiet strength.

ABOUT THE AUTHOR

Daniel Bay Gibbons is a writer living in Holladay, Utah. The youngest son of Francis M. Gibbons and Helen Bay Gibbons, he is a former trial attorney and judge and is the author of several previous books. He has served as a full-time missionary, twice as a bishop, and as president of the Russia Novosibirsk Mission.

INDEX

Allen, James, 25
Anderson, Elder
  Joseph, 34
As a Man Thinketh, 25
Ashton, Elder
  Marvin J., 54
Benson, President
  Ezra Taft
  death, 12
Boise, Idaho, 5, 15, 17, 37, 38
Bonneville Stake, 21, 35, 40
Bountiful, Utah, 13
Brigham Young
  University, 37
Broadhead, Daken
  K., 22
Brown, President
  Hugh B.
  as a lawyer, 19
Christopherson,
  Elder D. Todd
  as a lawyer, 19

Church
  Administration
  Building, 34
Church Historian, 10, 37
Clark, President J.
  Reuben
  as a lawyer, 19
Cove Fort, 38
Curtis, Marvin, 40
Douglas Ward, 40
Egypt, 8
Evans, Elder
  Richard L., 35
Faust, President
  James E.
  as a lawyer, 19
Fyans, Elder J.
  Thomas, 31
Genealogical
  Society, 9
Gibbons, Francis
  M.
  and HWH, 44

Granite Mountain
Record Vaults, 9
Grant, President
Heber J.
and Bryant S.
Hinckley, 39
Great Britain, 8
Hill, Napoleon, 25
Hinckley, Bryant
S., 39
Hinckley, Ira, 38
Hinckley, President
Gordon B., 36, 38
Holy Land, 8, 11
Hunter, Clara May
Jeffs, 6, 10, 18,
29
death, 10, 29
Hunter, Howard
William Jr., 6
Hunter, Inis
Stanton, 11
Hunter, John
William, 5
Hunter, Nellie
Rasmussen, 5
Hunter, President
Howard W.
and accident in
Egypt, 56
and Elder
LeGrand
Richards, 43
and Francis M.
Gibbons, 44
and SWK, 8
focus upon
Temple, 50
gives blessing to
childless
woman, 53
leadership style,
44
life
Apostolic
service, 8, 9,
10, 11, 12,
48, 53, 55
Apostolic
servicc, 37
birth, 5
call to the
Twelve, 8, 21
childhood, 5,
15, 17, 38

Church service, 7, 22
courtship, 6
death, 13
death threat, 12
education, 5, 6, 7, 39
family, 6, 10
health problems, 11, 13, 27
home, 49
legal career, 7, 19, 20
marriage to Clara May Jeffs, 6, 18
marriage to Inis Stanton, 11
musical career, 5, 6, 17, 18, 39
President of the Church, 12, 13
President of the Twelve, 11
life preserved, 56
love of music, 15
motto, 25
office of, 25
on Islam, 51
personal qualities
  cordiality, 44
  endurance, 28
  faith, 33
  faithfulness, 29
  genuineness, 36
  hopefulness, 28
  humor, 27
  independence, 15
  kindness, 33, 50
  love of books, 25
  love of children, 46
  musical talent, 16
  quiet strength, 58
  sense of humor, 46

spirituality, 53, 58
studious nature, 16
vision, 31
prophecy regarding LeGrand Richards, 58
Hunter's Croonaders, 18, 39
Iraq, 8
Jerusalem Center, 11
Kimball, President Spencer W., 21, 51
and HWH, 8
motto, 26
Lee, President Harold B., 34
Los Angeles, California, 6
McConkie, Elder Bruce R.
as a lawyer, 19
McKay, President David O., 10, 22
Merrill, Elder Joseph F., 44
Mexico City, 10, 12
Middlemiss, Claire, 22
Millard Stake, 38
Monson, President Thomas S., 36
Monument Park First Ward, 40
Monument Park Second Ward, 40
Monument Park Stake, 40
Moyle, President Henry D.
as a lawyer, 19
Nauvoo, Illinois, 12
Nelson, William O., 57
North Thirty Third Ward, 40
Oaks, Elder Dallin H.
as a lawyer, 19

as BYU president, 37
Orlando, Florida, 13
Packer, President Boyd K., 36
Pasadena Stake, 44
Pasadena, California, 22
Peterson, Elder Mark E.
　accident in Egypt, 55
Peterson, Lamonte, 40
Polynesian Cultural Center, 9
Quorum of the Twelve, 23, 57
Revelation on Priesthood, 58
Richards, Elder LeGrand
　and HWH, 43
　illness, 57
Richards, President Stephen L.
　as a lawyer, 19

Romney, President Marion G., 21
Salt Lake Central Stake, 40
Salt Lake Temple, 18, 42
Smith, President Joseph Fielding, 34
Solemn Assemblies, 37
South Pacific, 53
Southwestern University, 6
St. George Temple, 37
St. George, Utah, 37
Stapley, Elder Delbert L., 35
Tanner, President N. Eldon, 34
Temple Square, 35
Temples, 13
Think and Grow Rich, 25
Thirty-Third Ward, 40

Upper Room of the Salt Lake Temple, 34, 42
  described, 35
Upper Room of the Temple, 58
Ursenbach, Brother, 17
Woodruff, President Wilford
  appearance in Upper Room, 58
World Conference on Records, 9
Yalecrest Ward, 35
Young, President Brigham
  on lawyers, 19

www.ingramcontent.com/pod-product-compliance
Lightning Source LLC
Chambersburg PA
CBHW071542080526
44588CB00011B/1754